Praise for *Even Further*

MW00698052

"In *Even Further West*, Eric Paul Shaffer weaves a garland of narrative and lyric eco-poems gathered from the fallen blossoms of his experiences in Hawai'i. After journeying through this book, you will see the illuminated depths of our sacred ecology, our boat of bones, our living breath."

--Craig Santos Perez, author of *From Unincorporated Territory*, and Winner of the 2011 PEN Center USA Literary Award for Poetry

"Shaffer is Hawaii's Thoreau. Of the usual imaginings of Hawai'i, these poems resist the normal temptations to pare it down to palm trees and white sands. While being grounded in paradise, Shaffer simultaneously guides you to someplace deeper, someplace holier. Insightful, elegant and unpretentious, these words will make you remember the thing inside that you born with, but lost the second you learned your name."

--Christy Passion, author of *Still Out of Place* and co-author of *No Choice But to Follow* (with Ann Inoshita, Juliet Kono, Jean Toyama)

"In *Even Further West*, Eric Paul Shaffer beautifully locates himself and the islands of Hawai'i by means of a pleasantly apocalyptical geography of heart and mind that reaches home "in the last of the light" to unveil for us in his witty and all-seeing lyricism "the voiceless and eventual work the dark does." These are poems you will want to reread again and again."

--Joseph Stanton, author of *A Field Guide to the Wildlife of Suburban O'ahu*, *Cardinal Points*, and *Things Seen*

"Like a cocoon, Eric Shaffer's new book of poetry transforms mundane moments and objects in nature into something transcendental, and the lines take flight from the page. In the title poem 'Even Further West,' he writes about finding a cardinal feather and a cowrie shell and says, 'Hold them till your mind changes.' Many of these poems may change your mind about the things you take for granted, maybe even the way you look at the world."

--Stuart Holmes Coleman, author of *Eddie Would Go* and *Fierce Heart*

"In *Even Further West*, Eric Paul Shaffer belies the self-critique that ends his poem 'Upcountry Overlook: Kula, Maui': 'I gawked at the furrowed sea and sun-scored red slopes, attentive// to the distant and dramatic, but not to significant lives / close at hand, within reach, and indifferent to our slow recognition.' While he knows well that 'the light is gone before we even know we need to see,' what he sees is instructive: we learn to appreciate the beauty of Maui, but also human pain. Among the most moving of these poems are those that allude to a broken relationship between father and son, and between the poet and himself. 'If ever there was a good time to pull a Hemingway,/ this is it,' he writes in a novena. He pulls back, declares, 'I'm not going anywhere,' and returns to writing poems attentive both to natural beauty and the compassion that comes of attending to it, as to 'the close at hand.'"

Susan M. Schultz, author of *Aleatory Allegories, Dementia Blog,* and the *Memory Cards* series, and editor of Tinfish Press

For Elisa —
Illumination from
the Islands —
with both eyes!
Best,
Eric

Even Further West

Poems

Eric Paul Shaffer

Published by Unsolicited Press
www.unsolicitedpress.com
info@unsolicitedpress.com

Unsolicited Press Books are distributed by Ingram.
Printed in the United States of America.

Attention schools and businesses: for discounted copies on large orders,
please contact the publisher directly.

Learn more about Eric Paul Shaffer at https://www.ericpaulshaffer.com.

Acquisitions Editor: Rubie Grayson
Editor: S.R. Stewart
Cover Image: Charles W. Winegarner

ISBN: 978-1-947021-17-4

Contents

"The islands are even further west than I thought."

--overheard in Lāhaina

i. ka lā

light, day, the sun, and the fin above the waves
announcing life below the surface

A Boat of Bones

I'm on the beach, building a boat of bones, the long ones
from legs and arms, stripped of meat, slick and shiny,

as white as the sand where I kneel. I lash the bones
with sun-bleached twine, yellow rope, and a black cord
braided from torn strands of seaweed abandoned by tides.

I wish I was alone, but the poet squats beneath a palm,
his precious pages on his knee, scribbling literature

and telling me how to build a boat of bones. I don't listen
as he mumbles through blistered lips words I'm thankful
not to hear. Yesterday, he said, "One builds a boat as he

builds a poem, stave by stave." That means nothing to me.
I'm building a boat of bones, but I'm not caulking gaps,
for there is no caulk but damp sand, and this boat is built

to sink, not to sail. I'm hungry, he's hungry, and he's sick,
and we're both sick of fish. His eyes are sunk in his skull,

and seared red flesh burns through tears in his sleeves.
I'm building a boat of bones as I scan the horizon, stranded
with a babbler in rags who scratches verse in dim lines

on moldy pages, writing poetry with seawater and a stick.
"That boat is not worthy of the sea," he says, and he means

the boat will never float. Surf nearly drowns his voice,
but not quite. I'm building a boat of bones, and the last

I lash to the stern will be the poet's bones. Then, I'll drag
the boat through dunes, set the keel on the sea, thrust the bow
forward on a foam of broken waves. The boat will become

its own anchor and sink like one. I'm building a boat
of bones for the long voyage into the depths between me

and where I wish I was. The last of the boat I see will be
the poet's bones, flickering white, blue, gone, as the boat
sounds the fathoms I alone escaped. I'm building a boat

of bones, and when that craft sinks, the poet will be gone.
I'll sit silent on the sand and watch the empty sea for sails.

The Edge of Where I'm Welcome

At the edge of where I'm welcome, I pause. In the surf, children call
and splash. Men tease each other with words and boards. Women
coax the sun to darken their curves. Waves break like the quick flow
of something molten. One boy writhes in the sand, making an angel
on the beach. Another overturns a bucket, a perfect cone of sand
in a row of others whose rims crumble as the sea seeps from within.

Before me is the wrinkled blue face of the unknown. The sea looks
friendly. After striding through the sun and scorch of sand, I will walk
into the cool surge of what I cannot see, to float on the rising and falling
of wind and waves. The water is clear until I reach the depth a man
        can stand, where seeing through the waves becomes a trial.

One needs a mask, a mouthpiece, and a hollow rod to look into the sea
as far as the clarity of the unknown allows. But before all that, I pause
at the energetic edge. Where the horizon curls are the riders of waves,
the stronger swimmers, and the clouds marking the end of the world

I know. I take a moment to remember I'm standing on an island
where friends, food, and fresh water flow, where all that supports me
is all I need. I consider my place before I walk into water that bears me

away from the ground I depend on, before my feet dangle, flashing
and pale, over the darker ranges of a sinking world I no longer know
as I swim further from shore. I stand here, reverent, for a moment,

at the edge of everything I know, before I walk into the clear mystery
        of the depths before me, depths that welcome me, but do not.

Someone Else's Beach

I discovered a beach abandoned on an empty drive along the north shore
of Maui. I parked by a fence of imported wire and oak posts and found
a path crossing someone else's land. Someone always owns the land

between me and the sea. I apologize. Waves spit and slapped on a steep
shore of round, black stones the size of my head and greater. Before me,
tides carved a coast of pocked lava spheres and smoothed them round
as random planets stacked to stock stars in a new galaxy. Each gleamed

in surf. Every stone became a dark mirror. There was little to reflect.
On the horizon, sea slashed sky, and the beach was barren. Even crabs
clicking over the stones were ghostly. Light passed through their claws,

and all lost their sideways ways, assuming colors from the sand and rock
they crossed. Under the urge of the moon, the sea shifted the stones
with each breaking, and the groans and sighs were as bleak as the break

between waters above and below. At the edge of the land, east and west,
the stone spheres descended to the sea, and I watched the light span noon
and night. Beyond the starved grass, waves worked at tiny, insistent tasks,
and I saw no sign of what I knew went on, the unseen work of wearing

away what is fixed. I wondered who might find me and ask what I was
doing as darkness filled the world. I was doing nothing, and I would
have no answer, and I would meet anger again, and again, I would ask

forgiveness. Yet I lacked the will to turn my back on the sea, to follow
my own backward steps through sand to the place I had left and locked
my wheels. I knew I should rise and go, but I thumbed the harsh edges

of time one whorl at a time and sensed a vague, gray beauty in a day left
to me by distant lords who had left the gate agape. I sat long in a place
not my own as day faded. When sea and sky were one, I left the world
        as the world was and stumbled to my car. In the headlights, I saw

a brand-new sign nailed to a split gray wooden post: NO TRESPASSING.
I understood, but I ignored the words. There were only two and so small.
The stars were the only other light, and the road barely opened as I passed.

Walking Zone

You walk beneath trees and a scatter of leaves in the wind from the coast,
　　　along elementary school walls gleaming with a fresh coat of paint.

Stenciled in yellow Army-block letters on the institutional green
　　　cinderblock of the school are the words: "WALKING ZONE."

And in that capital font of command, they certainly look like yet another
　　　golden rule, not just a suggestion, but a proclamation,

a decree, a law of paint and plumbing and chain-link fences between youth
　　　and the roads that lead away. When the brazen bells clang,

you struggle to hold yourselves back as you hurry or dawdle
　　　or saunter along the grass and crisscross walkways

　　　　　　between classroom or cafeteria, the library or playground,
the nurse's or the principal's office, your energy crackling within,

　　　　　bones brilliant, blood gleaming, youth snapping from your soles
to the concrete, radiating visibly and transparently as light from the sun

　　　　　propagates the nourishing and dangerous heat of the day.
You file along the paths, straight in your gaits, and I wonder

　　　　at your fortitude, your dedication to keep the peace and the pace,
when you restrain that bold, emergent force, that rude urge, that wild drive

　　　　　to fling yourselves head-first into the future as everything
inside you demands that you run, commands you to run. To run. Run.

The Way of Feet

Anonymous and bony, essential to earth,
feet are faces familiar to the planet, the way
                    the place in the world we know

knows us before we know where we are.
Soil to sole, feet are a fundamental stretch
                    of our own flesh we never see, balanced

on steel rails, concrete curbs, rock or rungs.
I wouldn't recognize my own feet
                    if they weren't attached to the legs

I locomote along the spectacular
and elliptical paths I draw from darkness.
                    I scan my steps for rattlesnakes, scorpions,

sea urchins, watch for splintered glass,
rusty steel in boards weathered gray,
                    and the lazy rake on the lawn. I scrub

my feet in the surf, wander through sand,
wipe them on the grass, thoughtless.
                    I tend the nails as an afterthought. My toes

are a joke for my fingers to mock. I stride
with my feet like a flame over the fields,
                    my twin devourers of blue distance,

my tough underlings marking my pace,
my two ravagers of the open spaces spun
                    within horizons no journey conquers.

For My Sake

There was no line at the bookstore. At noon, I read
at the register. My only customer was a dying man,

his flesh gone, his skin like badly-folded, purple-
blotched paper on a gift to someone no one likes.

He shuffled to the counter beneath a weight of books,
his grin a gritting of teeth set in a permanent task.

When we think of heavy books, we think two or three
unabridged dictionaries carried against the chest.

Not this time. This man tottered with a two-foot stack
of paperbacks, each an inch or two or less thick.

He wheezed, searching pockets for cash and coins
as red light read commercial codes through glass.

The titles were astonishing: *How to Defend Yourself
Against Alien Abduction, A Gift from the Sea,*

*The Wicked Stone, The Pocket Catholic Dictionary,
The Millionaire Mind, How to Take Better Black*

*and White Photographs, All I Ever Really Needed to Know
I Learned from My Horse, 10,001 Baby Names,*

Guns, Germs, and Steel, and thirty-seven others.
I smiled and said, "That's a lot of reading."

He said only, "I'll get it done," and refused
my offer to carry his books into the rain.

He was determined to get those books home,
determined to do it on his own and alone.

If there were a God, I would order him
to bless this man. But as the universe seems

to be on its own, I will only hope someday
my customer reads this poem, recognizes himself,

and smiles, not because he needs to know
someone saw him once and stole his life

as words for these lines, but for my sake.

An Inflatable Globe for Your Birthday

for Conner

This is how we see the world in the third millennium, with the eyes
of astronauts, suspended in stars on a long arc through darkness.

The continents of red and gold and green are bordered by seas as big
and blue as always, trimmed with whorls and curls of white weather

and wind. What you see is nearly a sphere, without the lines we draw
in the sand and through seas to separate us. This is the whole world

and the world whole, a globe that welcomes all, ages zip to infinity.
Every day, the round orb shines. Take the ball to the beach. Watch

the globe roll on the shore or bounce on the crests of breaking waves.
At night, after a day in the sun, our cities glow with the light we make

for ourselves. Hug the planet and dream. Now, and in days to come,
the world is in your hands. Care for it. Keep it safe. Astonish yourself

with its rugged, gentle grace. Let ours become your favorite planet.
Whether you think of Earth as a big blue marble or a pale blue dot

in a limitless cosmos, here it is: a world to fill with your living breath.

Cardinal in February: Oʻahu

When I see a cardinal in February, I think of snow
        even as I stand on a green lawn beneath palms
and plumeria, watering the grass. I think the bird

must wonder where the long drifts of winter are,
for once, days grew shorter, and snow was inescapable.
        When the others fled south, flying in martial V's

and raucous flocks to follow summer, the cardinals
remained, linked to the land in a way that denied seasons
and weather and want. Cardinals were as rooted to place

        as any maple, oak, or elm I remember in all
the places I've forgotten. Some human caged and carried
enough cardinals to the tropics that here is one, bold

and red, his striking song ringing from a telephone wire.
And now, he lights on the ground in a silvered circle
        of morning grass, and because I cannot

not think his thoughts, I think he thinks, "Yes, this is it.
        Here I am." The rainbow in the spray can't touch
the crimson of his wings. Even marooned on Oʻahu,

the cardinal cannot care, yet I am as transfixed by his red
on this green as I once was by his scarlet in the snow.
        Pulling a hardy weed, I'm the one who wonders

about the fading drifts of yesteryear, the one who walked
        away from place after place to find another place.
I turn the spigot, coil the hose, and wipe away my sweat.

Now, his mate flits to the fence, bronze and watchful,
silent as he skips through a slanting ray of winter sun
        over ground he claims with only a shadow.

Witnesses

These two women call themselves witnesses. Desire drives
               them to speak of a place they cannot describe
without words someone else placed in their mouths. A mynah

         squawks somewhere near, but everything else is still.
Even the road is silent. The door between us is locked.
           I smile at them through the screen, but I will not allow

them to enter, though the scent of roses fills the air between us.
         The bush by the porch is blooming. Neither the sun
nor the drought nor whatever chews holes in new green leaves

         can kill that tough stalk of thorns. These women yearn
to speak of saviors on a day when the concrete is mute at noon
           and the air too parched to spin a mirage from the ridge.

         I know enough of kindness to leave them
to their tragic metaphysics. One I love is dying, and these two

         know nothing of grief when death is final, immutable,
irrevocable. Heat like this might teach them if they were more
           than only lonely, and even traveling together, alone.

Above their upturned faces, the wasps work at the nest, mold
               a living beneath the eaves from paper and spit,
and these women hover now near my door as if at any moment

they might embark on a flood-borne vessel. The temperature
         stands at 88. They carry pamphlets and scripture bound
in hope and cowhide. No matter what they say, I'll never know

         more of hell than they will. Behind them, weeds are
the only green in a field scorched grim and gold. The sky is blue
         flame, and the mountain bears the light like a burden.

Redemption

Someone convinced me that to praise Jesus, I should visit someone
languishing in jail, so I slunk my way downtown to Oh-Triple-See.
For all anybody knows, those letters could mean Oklahoma City
Community College or even Orange County Conservation Corps,
but they don't. They mean Oʻahu Community Correctional Center.

The barbed wire and concrete walls are on a boulevard in Honolulu,
catty-corner from a recycling and redemption place: a nickel, a can.
I guess redemption keeps the streets fairly clean. That's a good thing.
So there I was. The clanging and slamming of steel was as musical

as it was peaceful. At random, a cheerful guard picked me a prisoner,
one with no visitors since intake. Frisked and X-rayed to invisibility,
I stared through lipstick-smudged, bullet-proof glass at one mean guy.
What could I say? I picked up the phone. So did he, a weird mirror
of reflections, shifting, and bent elbows. Warned to avoid the personal,

my tongue was tied to details of his incarceration, and they weren't
pretty. Grand larceny, drugs, domestic abuse: this guy was no friend
to Jesus, and not to me either. He asked what the hell I was doing here.
I wanted to know, too, so I asked him what *he* thought. He thought

I was an asshole or a fag. All his sentences included the word "fuck"
three or four times as a noun, verb, adjective, adverb, or interjection,
and I'm not used to that sort of language. Few words actually function
fully as five parts of speech. He just didn't care. To kill some time,
I asked him what *he* wanted, and he asked me what the hell I thought

he wanted. I was justifiably piqued by then, so I guessed he wanted
a li-hing-mui-sprinkled cherry slush from Byron's because I was sure
that's what I wanted. He was surprised, but then ardently advised me
to encounter myself sexually. By then, I'd had enough bad humor,

so I hung up and stood up. He banged his erect middle finger loudly on the glass, and I wondered if the print on that very tip was the one to clinch his conviction. How ironic. He ordered me to stay, I left, and he cursed me because I could. Jesus or not, I had done my time. In my trunk, I'd crammed three reeking garbage bags of empty cans.

On the Set of *Lost*

Dillingham Boulevard, Honolulu

Iraq was erected behind faculty parking on an ungraded gravel lot
　　　　backed by trashed and abandoned low-income apartments.
Storefronts rose from plaster, chicken wire, peach paint, and universal
applications of dirt and dust for verisimilitude. Eddie told me all about it.
　　　　　　Some set artist chose Arabic characters at random
from a font palette and dabbed them on facades. Authentic gibberish.

　　　Easy fakery was on my mind when my quietest student spoke
in class today. "9/11 was a hoax," he said. "It never really happened."
　　　　　For once, I was without words, but another spoke,
"Tell that to the people staring into space where two towers used to be."

My brother-in-law Eddie kept his plastic Kirkwood water bottle hidden
　　　　　　　　in a bogus bombed-out car by the imaginary roadside.
He introduced me to his thin, demure wife for the day, so silent, so gaunt,
　　　　　　　　so unlike my happy, affectionate sister. Did this woman
wrapped in black look as women look in Iraq, or did she simply mock
　　　　our notions of what we imagine she looks like on those streets?

I doubt that. Disbelief is no longer willingly surrendered, but eagerly
　　　　　　and widely applied to horrendous events that overcome us.
We'd rather believe an autopsy of aliens recovered in Socorro, drawn
and quartered in Quonset huts secreted in Area 51, than believe
　　　　any of us can do to the rest of us what has been done to all of us.

　　　The scene is shot and shot and shot and shot and shot again,
every movement repeated for the same camera rolling forth and back
on temporary tracks. Authentic reinforced-concrete rubble was trucked in
　　　　　　from the remodeling of a Waikīkī five-star resort.
Near every ice-filled orange cooler, smudge pots were set, to dim Heaven
　　　　　　　　with smoke as dark as the sky must be in Iraq.

E-mails from the production crew invited the college faculty
                    to watch filming on Friday. Eddie was an Iraqi
                extra in the scene, so I slipped beneath the yellow tape
and stood in aloha shirt, faded jeans, and sneakers in a desert market
            while the crew yelled instructions to their $75-a-day flock.

        The only talent on the set was Sayid, chain-smoking in shadows
with the pallbearers or hustling to the director and high crew to view
                        the replay before the scene was shot once more.
All the money and time in the world were spent to film this snippet
            as many times as needed to get it right, to get it plausibly faked.

                    In the aired episode, I see Eddie cross the street
as the coffin approaches. Later, he paces the dusty marketplace
            in a quick view from above. Then, there is one moment,
                when the camera pans past him, and I advance frame
by frame, he turns almost far enough for me to be sure his face is his.

In such expensive attention to the smallest detail, however faithless
                    the reality of the set, there must be something true
filmed in all this faking. It looks so real on TV. Desert dust swirls around
my brother-in-law, the U.S. mail-carrier, an Iraqi-for-a-day. There must be
                    some truth in appearances, and whatever it is
must be what makes Hollywood a shrine and paves a sidewalk with stars.

The casting director told his Iraqi crew they might be recalled
            for filming further flashbacks, and Eddie says he will return
to the ersatz desert, though the wrecked apartments will be razed this year.
Iraq will be moved elsewhere in paradise, yet the details--real, invented,
                and faked--will all surely look real enough to be true.

Upcountry Overlook: Kula, Maui

The ancient picnic table is a rotting wreck in rattling gray grass
        stiff in the season of slow growing. Nothing greens here

without a gift of water. Weeks burn by, and the stalks grow only
gold in the glare. Behind me, the sun casts a slant of silver rays
        through clouds, over fields of sugar cane, on the ridges

        and gulches to the west. From above, a sifting of leaves
and dust of bark from the kiawe tree litters the boards. Motes spark
        in the sun warming my back like the hand of an old friend

        come early. No one else has ever seen this place this way,
this morning, this moment, nor will they again. The sun moves,

the clouds wander. When I raise my cup, the coffee is burred
        with floating bits, a black deeper in the sudden light. I pitch
the last of the lukewarm brew over the grass and set down the mug.

        Then, I see the scorpion, green as the table's peeling paint,
a handspan from my fingers still looped through the cup's ring.

        Bees hover and birds bounce through thick limbs overhead,
but a scorpion's poise reveals its presence. Maybe since I arrived

with pen, paper, and an eye for the view, it's been coiled there
        like a threat, an accident awaiting the witless. All morning,
I gawked at the furrowed sea and sun-scored red slopes, attentive

        to the distant and dramatic, but not to significant lives
close at hand, within reach, and indifferent to our slow recognition.

Maybe

Every second upcountry Sunday morning, she cuts
my hair in the tilting driveway beneath our little piece
of sky: it just must be done. Gray above, wet grass.

Rain fell all through the night, and when I dressed
to lug trashcans to the street, I saw not a single light
in any direction. Fog muffled my steps and the stars,

hid all beyond the gray haze. Ours was the only light
in the world. The little hair I have falls to the grass
and concrete like scales from weathered stone, darker

on the ground than on my skull. Now, the rain starts
again. A few drops rattle the roof. Then, all at once,
the tin rings, and the horizon shrinks to a silver circle

girding the house, the car, and us. A butterfly passes,
bobbing through the downpour as though the rain
means nothing, and maybe it does, maybe it does.

All There Is

an epithalamion for Jon and Thierry

Winter in paradise this year is dry enough to call a drought.
    The grass isn't green and isn't growing in the season

    we call the rainy one. No clouds color sunrise,
and every night, stars deepen the sky. Ancient light rains
from cloudless darkness. If there were enough for everyone,

    the rays wouldn't travel so fast. Light is a constant
reminder of the yearning between stars and all the worlds

    spinning in darkness, like this one, the one we love.
For this brown grass and the open space between stars,
    there's not much rain. Never will there be too much

or even enough, so we celebrate and celebrate fiercely
    all there is. When the rain finally comes, I'll stand

in the storm with my face raised. When the night comes,
I'll lift my eyes to the light and take it in. Rain will grace us,
    and stars will burn. Light flies through the night,

and rain finds the earth for no reason we know, yet we leap
    to drink our fill of what falls from above to sustain us.

ii. ke ahiahi

dusk, evening, the time when torches are lit

Letter to Slow Cooker in Colorado

Aloha, kākou:

Holy crap, I stand at rain-streaked windows on the third day
of the first semester of the second decade of the third millennium (enough
numbers to stun me and my students). The glass ripples with windy spray
in a city sunk in muddy puddles and running gutters.

Today, in class, we read Shakespeare's "Sonnet 29." I smiled
(as I always do) when the man wishes he were "like him with friends
possess'd," because he means *me*, one whose world rings within a great
circle of friends. Shakespeare, I tell them, is dead, but that doesn't stop
him from speaking with a living tongue thrumming along the lines he left
us. Lucky? You bet he is, and so am I. Remember? You named me "Lucky"
on the day I left to live in the pacific, little nation whose language left me
stunned and stuttering.

Here, mountains are young, green, and grooved. Gods house
the sun on the one I worship. At night, lightning flickers over an ocean
lost in clouds. There's no more to say: I, too, have no words for my father.
Words are too lame and too lazy to bear the weight across the roiling blue
beneath storm and stars. Our fathers drove us far away, and as the man
said, "I will fight no more forever." Men bear too little of the grief
and burdens of the world. We can wish them strength, but most lack
the courage to claim even that.

I'm sad to hear of the suicides, young and old. So many mean
to murder us, the wonder is that we will commit the act ourselves. All of us
are coming apart. I may spit a tooth tomorrow if the root still rocks
in the socket. That will put a spin on my grin, eh?

Jupiter rose only minutes after midnight, and by the way, happy
birthday. After 20,000 dawns and companion sunsets, you deserve one.
I wish you one, and nobody can take that away. No matter how damned
many years ago you or I or Johnny D. were born, never will we see enough
days to properly celebrate lives we neither expected nor deserved.

May the new year sparkle. The future is upon us, and I,
with the two of you, will cast wide the wooden gates
on rusted hinges, and let the light fall where it may.

All for now,

Reckless

Headlights: A Biology Lesson

The sun gone, the green in the fields darkens. My neighbors drive on
without headlights, as if dusk were clouds of cane smoke and their vision
was improved by speeding past the burning stalks. Mr. Brown, our teacher
of biology and Drivers Ed., once asked our class a question,

"What are headlights for?" Someone snorted and said, "So you can see
where you're going." Mr. Brown scowled. That wasn't what he wanted,
so he tried again, "What is the most important use of headlights?"
When he put it that way, no one spoke. Everyone recognized a trap.

He rocked on his toes, waited long, and then gave us the words he wanted:
"So other drivers can see *you*."
But speeding through oncoming night, these drivers don't want to see me.
They want to see an open road, a wild land, a new world, a paradise paved

for their wheels alone. Night conquers the world, and they want to think
they know where they're going. The cars, glossy but without color,
are no longer visible. Nobody can see them, and they can't see each other.
They fly over darkling land, crossing double yellow lines on blind curves

so they need not break the homeward rush. At my approach, the sullen flick
their parking lights to say, "I don't *need* lights. I can see."
Maybe day fades at such a petty pace they fool themselves that they *can* see.
The road is familiar. They know every curve and dip, every weedy ditch

and flower-covered cross along the way. Most nights, they don't remember
driving home as they arrive, so they truly believe they don't need the light.
But I am cursed to recall Mr. Brown's brutal biology lesson,
the one where the frog lolls in a beaker of cool water with a thermometer

and a Bunsen burner below. The temperature rises gently to a killing boil,
so the frog never senses danger and slowly, stupidly cooks in the cauldron.
Driving home tonight, I see that's how darkness works, too: so gradually,
the light is gone before we even know we need to see.

Telephone Lines

When the telephone first came to our upcountry farm in Kula,
there was only one wire. The numbers were a digit different,

but it was the same line. When anybody's rang, ours rang
in the kitchen, and so rang the receivers in every other house.
No matter what somebody said, anybody could be listening,

and everybody knew it, so nobody ever said anything important
or personal on the phone. Phones were public like a restroom

or a library is public. If the words were private, they were taken
outside or penned. Nobody ever called anybody for no reason,

and conversations were short. Before the telephone, we lived
alone where we couldn't even see the neighbors' lights at night,
but the wires shrunk the world. No longer was there anywhere

you knew anybody you couldn't call anymore. So we called.
Whenever we picked up the phone, there were voices in the line.

Weather Eye

Every night, the weatherman proves he does not understand weather.
He thinks clouds symbolize sadness. He thinks seven months of sun
is good weather and looks grim when he finally announces a rainy day.

My grass is gray, and the hibiscus withers, and he weeps to unfurl
an umbrella. Weather is not the mood of the world, though he'd like

to make it so. Weather is what we discuss instead of incest, murder,
the end of the world, or the arrival of one more child as a witness.

Snow, rain, fog, and sun are weather, the short season the day wears,
constant and changing, yet when we ignore calm blue or windless dark,
we forget weather that neither diverts nor distracts us is weather, too.

On My Father's Wish That I Not Attend His Funeral

The miles are long between us, but I will cross them
and the baleful, blue sea, the drifting sand scattered
with days, and the mountains keen enough to draw

my heart to a sky widening with every wheel and wing
I apply to the angry distance. If only to cross you
in your sulky last wishes, I will fly to where you lie,

a small corpse in a cheap casket. I am the elder son,
and my job is to dispose of you in the modest manner
you deserve. I see you dead on a rare day of rain

in empty desert beneath a sky with little room for God
but large enough to hold a will even as large as yours.
I will come and stand at last before a narrow gathering

of eyes who have come to close yours, who have come
to dust your face with dirt, to drop a pale, prickless rose
on the beaming coffin lid, and I will speak your truth.

What Rain Brings to the Volcano

What rain brings to the volcano is welcome darkness, thin rivulets
        of water shaping rock once molten, sudden streams on slopes
once forged by fire and flow and a call within the earth, a veil

        of white slowly descending dry, golden slopes, a cool reprieve
from summer sun, a silence from birds and tractors working
           the fields, a pinging, a drumming, a deafening thunder

on a corrugated roof, water enough to slap the world awake
        with green, the unexpected return of light to a day gone gray,
an ever-so-slightly new shape for the peak, a cap of clouds

        covering the crest, the lisping whine of wheels past the house,
a lone truck descending the hill, the sun emerging, steam rising
        from the road's dark face, a muggy heat driving me to shade,

a rasp and scatter of insects born in a new, wet landscape,
          and silver scales on every leaf of grass I must mow.

On the Day the World Ends

On the day the world ends, I want rain, one of the relentless
downpours in Kula, with dark clouds crowning the mountain
and to the west, sun blinding on a blank ocean edged by the black

slope of the volcano. I want a white sky on a late October
afternoon when summer grass at last begins to blaze emerald
      from a few lazy showers after long, dry weeks, and the hibiscus

holds only a few half-blown red blooms and one of the weird,
          white ones that opens from time to time on the branch

I never trim. I want big drops banging like mad liquid hammers
      on the corrugated roof of the carport while water pounds

the ground with thick silver, igniting the glow in the grass
and buffing mirrors in the mud. Deafened to music and news,
      I want to watch clouds over the coast wind through the wind

      in a sky without a trace of blue. I want to see the sun slant
under the clouds at the undeniable angle that burns a rainbow

        on leaden clouds behind the house, but I will not turn
to gaze at that last deceptive slash. On the day the world ends,

I will face the road where cars slow on curves below my house
      and see their diamond headlights flash as tires jolt
through tears in black tar and send the light flying. I will be home

on a wordless vigil with the ones I love, watching the last
      cars hiss over steep, wet road as my neighbors
rush by, weeping, desperate to reach home in the last of the light.

What I'll Miss When I'm Gone

I will miss the light. The south windows allow the sun to fill the rooms
from morning to dusk. After all, without light, there is little to see, wall
to wall, window to door, ceiling to floor, nothing but nothing but darkness.

And I will miss the way the light stands on the neat boards of the floor
and looks around, a gaze bounding round the room, reflecting only
on every surface and revealing all the corners and angles that the sun will.
I'll miss the height of the house. Not that I like to look down on people,

but my walls and windows are high on the ridge, raised on wooden beams
and crossbeams so that the roofs of other houses are far below where I sit
gazing at the sea. And I will miss the freighters anchored off the coast,

especially at night when they light themselves like small islands on a grand,
barren, black plain, golden orbs gleaming between me and the horizon,
drawing my attention to where the world happens. The ridge of the valley

that rises like the great, green face of a wave, I will miss. A soaring surge
of earth, still moving but fixed before my eye, that ridge reminds me always
that nothing in this valley will long remain. And I will miss the coconut tree
poised before the largest window, blocking the view of the streets below

with little scenes of sparrows, doves, and bulbuls of every song, strand,
and scrappiness. And I suppose I'll miss the days when I'm home, and all
the noisy neighbors are working or playing far away, and that blessed,

vacant, and resonant calm steeps in the sun and shade on the tilted lane
and clustered houses. And I'll miss flights of jets blasting from the airport,
spiking to the zenith in a dull rumble of rush and arrogance. I'll miss that

weird pattern of roofs, the oddly-chosen colors and alternating shimmer
on shingles when all the angles change as the sun crosses the sky. And I will
certainly miss the nights, when I rise, barefoot, and glide to early windows
over a silent valley sprinkled with the lights of the restless and the negligent,

and above that lonely, electric pattern on the darkness of the earth are stars, telling mythic stories, unread by eyes that can't see beyond their own walls and raised roofs, locked doors, curtained windows, and purchased light.

The Floor God

When glasses tip, silverware falls,
> or the wheel of carrot rolls in a lazy arc
that ends beneath the stove, we think of him
> as mischievous, a tease, a sulky brat
whose antics knock things down. We conceive

a squat, bow-legged dwarf whose pale, relentless,
> rippling arms drag down the ripe, the ruined,
and the rain. In the kitchen, he even seems
> homely, but he's at home throughout the world,
floor and sidewalk, road, field, waves, and peak.

Our indifference masks his majesty, yet he is a god
> to whom all things fall, first and foremost,
from hand, from table, from lip, from roof,
> from sky. Drawing apple to Earth, he knotted
Newton's skull. His grip gives meaning

to the mountain's struggle to pierce the blue.
> He hugs his mother's girth and pats
the pregnant planet round, as bigger brothers
> gather dust in glowing balls to burst into suns.
To many, he seems serious, sullen, subtle,

even grave, liable to a thousand under-handed
> tricks, yet he graciously stages our comedy
within curved horizons revealing the good-natured
> grin of one who knows us all from heel to toe.
He is the tranquil god whose domain is down,

his face, the surface where sky starts, where sole
              meets earth, where we stand and raise our gaze
to stars. He was first to help us to our feet
          and gives our dreams direction, the humble god
of ground we rarely honor, to whose deeps

there is one end alone, from whom all arise and to whom
          all must fall. Let the odd luck of living inform
our praise, as we offer our sudden, swift attention
                  to chance and the scattered alms of accident
when we spill our milk or wine or blood.

My Potatoes, Too

for Mason, Evan, and all my foolish ancestors

We chant our childish song of counting.
One by one, at dusk, the little fists fall.
One by one, we hit on who is "out."

     "One potato, two potato . . . ,"

Below are my feet, bare on beaten
earth. Dirt does not discriminate.
Where we stand, the land marks us,
claims us with the tint of local soil.

A potato is a knot, a word of earth
the green forces forward. A root,
free, glad to flee dirt, leaps into light.

     ". . . three potato, four, . . ."

Potatoes are firm and round and brown,
     like me, a skin sparked with eyes,
open and distant and steady as stars.

Cut, to let in light, the flesh is white.
But whole, rolling, the heavy bodies
are filled with darkness, just like me.

     ". . . five potato, . . ."

None but those who mound mud suspect
the flower has a small, sweet scent,
and the fruit, should you eat, will kill.

That modest bloom, white or pale purple
atop the stubby stalk, suggests nothing
of the tough tuber born of the earth.

"...six potato,..."

We grow large in the light of the land,
like a hardy, hidden tumor, like an eye
in an embryonic skull, like a mote of dust

luring other motes to cluster and clump
and chunk, to embody a place, yet abide
            unseen, like a heart in the dark,
swelling with fear and breath and hope.

"...seven potato, o'er."

The knotted rock of fingers descends
            on mine. It's over. I'm out.
I place my fist behind my back.

Dogs, Men, and Fences in Fog

A fence spans a prairie fog,
a straight line in and out of nowhere,
                                taut wire and wood,
and pathless grass in all directions.

I'm sitting on a post, thinking
the human condition isn't so bad.
We've simply mystified ourselves
            with our own exquisite abstractions.

The world turns away from us,
astride oak posts and barbed wire,
            barriers built with our own hands
and tools we're too lazy to carry far.

The animals no longer understand us,
although many recall us fondly.
                    We believe them ignorant
enough to wait where wire meets wood.

We are apart, alone, in the fog
with only our dogs to lead us.
            We look to them for direction
when we start our way home.

Too Dark to Read

When it's too dark to read, I lower the book and look to the sky,
still blue and glowing, crimson and gold at the sea's far edge.
        Our little yellow star has sunk beyond the mountains.

Night rises behind me. Bugs whir in the grass. Trees are black
        against the sky, but on the ground, grass is faintly silver.

The sky reveals not a single star, the open blue blank at day's end.

Sun gone, wind crowds the dusk with thick, green scents of life.
        Without light for the pages, I watch the world darken.

You asked me to call you for the first star, and I watch the sky
from my weathered chair. The brightest pierces deepening blue
        at last, and I call you out to see what darkness illuminates.

Sitting in the Last of Sunset,
Listening to Guests Within

All my friends are in the kitchen now. Dinner is done, the sun set,
and after our muted admiration from the yard, by ones and twos,
they rose beneath a sky gone dull and turned to the house for wine

or coffee and pie. Plates clatter, and cabinets bang, and the spigot
gurgles in the sink. I'm alone on the last step, watching universal
blue darken the mountains and the sea. Over all, the voices carry

laughter through the windows open to the cool. As I sit here,
I'm laughing as they laugh, and the night unveils the keen eyes
piercing the sky deepening beyond my gaze. I'm content at the end

of a day of joy. A new bottle is uncorked, and from within, they call
my name. The stars are far, the moon far from full, yet even alone
under these old stars, I'm not alone. Now is the moment to return

to warm, yellow rooms crowded with companions, to leave the owl
hovering silent over the fallow field and the ten thousand tongues
of the starlit trees to the voiceless and eventual work the dark does.

iii. ka pō

night and the rich darkness from which all life
and creation emerge

Samson

The number 20 bus through Honolulu was nearly empty when I boarded.
Two men and a woman were the only passengers, all seated as far
from each other as they could get. I sat in the first forward-facing seats
on the right, slouching sideways and lazily regarding my reflection

in the opposite window. Through my face passed streetlights and traffic
signals and beer signs and strip club marquees and, many times, the word
"OPEN." The day had been good. Work was done and done well,
and now, a promise of soft light and wine drew me home. From the last

row of the bus, one of the men rose and walked toward me. He was thick
with muscle, tribal tattoos, brown from the sun, and his hair was long,
curly and black. He slid into the next seat and stared. "I'm Samson,"
he said, "I had to come up here." I nodded and told him my name, too.

We swayed along in silence for a few blocks. His profile was as noble
as his name, and even in ghostly light, his skin was the color of a handful
of honey. "I have to know," he went on, "What are you smiling about?"
I laughed. "Was I smiling?" He nodded. "You were." I watched fast-

food signs and headlights and dim storefronts slide through our reflections.
"It's been a good day, Samson." He gazed at the front windows of the bus
and the dark boulevard. "Yeah?" he said. Then, convinced, with a nod,
he said, "Yeah." And together, we passed through the pillars of the night.

Streamside

He bought the house because the stream obliquely crossed the corner
        of the dog-eared lot. Extending the property lines from the south
and west made the rocky bed a bit of his place. He wanted to own

a part of the flowing and the current, a corner whose contents swelled
in the rainy season and through the rest of the year sank under rounded,

        heated stones beneath the sun. He wanted a piece of the water
constantly coming and going, descending and meandering, making a way
through the world directed by tilt and terrain. He saw in the stream

        a casual thoughtless progress meaningful only to an eye and mind
stumbling into an unexpected weedy glade. Leaning on the chain-link

and gazing into the water might free him from the spectacle of minutes
        dragging themselves with large and little hands through the hours.
He knew he couldn't own a stream, but the illusion that one triangular snip

was his was enough. He would climb down the stacked rocks, stand
        ankle-deep in a flow flickering with sunlight and breathe the green

that leans across the way of water. He would see the light of the moon,
        if not the silver face, in the midnight darkness on whirling water,
                and forget the running stream would not reflect the stars.

A Constant Line of Ants Through Night

Ants stream beneath the sill, purposeful and mindless of the world
that only seems greater than they are. Walls and trees loom above,

and ants work, always, at whatever they work on. Taking trash
to the shed, I watch beneath a bulb paled by night as the ants draw

a constant line along the wall below my door. The stars are brilliant,
but the ranks of ants travel through the limitless dark, the little chill,
the magnificence of night that diminishes me, but to ants means nothing.

Steadily, they enter the hill whose purpose they serve but do not know
they do not know. Their vision is strict and short, and what we call
the universe is a grand blank emptiness of no interest, unless to serve

the worthy in a distant chamber, to carve an empty art of endless
galleries from earth whose presence is its purpose, to walk tunnels

whose surfaces are their only significance, because what is beyond
ants is never questioned, and before them, there is work to be done.

The Lone Streetlight on Piliwale Road

I'm supposed to say something like light
defeats darkness and beats back the shadows,
but from the bottom of the road, the radiance
is a dull smudge on black. There's nothing
noble in the little bit of illumination the lone
streetlight spills on this short black strip
of Piliwale Road.

          The stars are bold, blue,
and the edge of the galaxy burns through
the sky, every brilliant point, another ray
cast into the vast void where all light is lost.

I'm supposed to wish for dawn and see hope
in the day that conceals stars in a blue mask,
to find solace in the tragedies and comedies
we make of our lives as we make ourselves
the measure of all things.

              As I drive
up the hill, the light from the bulb swells
into a dim golden ring with ragged edges
of grass and a scatter of plumeria blossoms.
In that pale glow, the spit of road is brief,
a span of black from nowhere to nowhere
and gone.

          I'm supposed to celebrate
the victory of light, but I just can't see one.
There is nothing more here than a faint fire,
a spark with no strength against the night,
and nobody will miss that light less than I will
when somebody finally blasts that bulb blind.

A Humanity of Glass

words too late for my grandfather

All crave an end to light, but we people of glass
need simply sprint at stone and shatter bone
        to silver splinters, or torch our homes,
heat ourselves within to a fierce, orange glow,

then dive into winter lakes, or smash our temples
with ugly chunks of quartz. For people
        of glass, fragility is the first fact,
and there is no hiding our shared brittle frailty.

But kin to windows, who would wish for death?
In our humanity of glass, hearts are transparent.
        Thoughts are clear. Like the sun,
we cannot conceive darkness, know no shadow

of our own. Warmed by sunlight, we are content,
for appearance means nothing to crystalline skin.
        Through the limpid bodies of others,
we see clouds, stars, trees, rocks, rivers, sunsets,

and roses as clearly as we see through ourselves.
Needless, mirrors reflect only on their surroundings,
        and featured simply for clarity,
our vanity fills only footprints left on beaches

as we walk through lucid days. Our footprints
appear, one after the other, in a shining line
        wandering the opaque, shifting
stuff of ourselves, our ancestors, our children.

Within the waves, we open an eye in the tides
for glimpses of coral and starfish, the shark's fin,
                and the blue muscle of the sea.
Diamonds, our wealthy cousins thrice removed,

are best friend to none and known as the distant,
vulgar relatives they are. Our hands hide
                nothing of the roses they hold.
And among people of glass, there is no suicide.

Seeing through each other is a simple matter,
no secrets, no hates harbored in darkness,
                no pettiness seething in our skulls.
Each beams in the sun, minds and hearts open

to the passage of light flying through our minds,
flowing through our hearts like water, touching
                the earth without casting
our own thick, dark images to the ground.

In cascades of light, people of glass are nothing,
and we know well the way the world looks without us.
                Yet when flesh is glass, eyes
are crystal, and we people of glass are blind,

for only in darkness does light become vision.
Empty of all but light, we know only darkness.
                Blind in a paradise invisible to us,
as we are invisible, we move as wind moves.

Invincible to thorns, we know roses only
as they open, petal by petal. Finding each other
                is luck, and love, no longer a mystery,
becomes a shadow we cannot cast, leaving us

only sunlight and shining voices in crystal air.

Picnic in the Year Zero

Beyond the blue blanket, the horizon disappears. The sea
and the sky blur in the air, and the island drifts like a cloud of rock
lost in two thousand miles of ocean,

sixty miles of sky, and light years so vast there is no room
among the stars for Heaven, or that journey nobody wants to begin
alone. Above the tide, on the sand, we spread

the cloth and set the meal. We carry what we're taught
to carry: a basket with bread, wine, cheese, greens, and sweets.
And we stake our claim to a shore far from sunset

on the last day anyone will ever call nineteen-anything.
As I remember the day, the real excitement was at midnight.
Our eyes shone as we waited for the world

to end. The globe slid down the pole in the cold.
We cheered for night to last and year to lapse. Standing shoulder
to shoulder in the square, we urged the power to fail,

time to stop, and darkness to fall. Yes, we long for apocalypse,
how we burn to be there, to witness the world's end,
to feel fiery tongues lick life away, so that not only does everybody

die, but everybody dies with us. No saviors, no survivors.
Apocalypse was much easier in the Atomic Age. Ray Milland
steered his sculpted tons of Detroit steel to his secret

mountain hideaway, shepherding his fleeing family
of Adams and Eves madly before the flash marking the end
of everybody else. He was a noble Noah,

commanding his ship of stone. Mankind overboard. Damn
the torpedoes. Full speed ahead. But the ball exploded into light.
The bulbs burned on, illuminating a new millennium.

Sentiments for all ages blared through public address,
and life went on, and on, and on again. We stomped back to the bar
for more to drink, more to eat, more to do before doom comes

one by one to each of us, end after end, after all, into the gloom alone.
Slapping backs, blowing on our hands, we all know
we're solo on a lone road to the ultimate. Nothing can save us.

Now, after bread, cheese, and wine with a view, it's easy to let it go.
I'm not bold, just lazy. If the end is near,
let me greet it here, near a beach where waves whisper lies

about eternity, and night reveals the stars
are as insignificant as we are, where wind guides the sand
in the only direction time allows, where I can step

from this shore into a blessed blankness beyond light,
icy heavens, and a God we've fooled ourselves into believing,
where one spark disappears at last

into the absolute darkness that extinguishes all
I think of when I think of me, and let the day be done.

To Write on the Moon

When he said he wanted to write on the moon,
she thought he meant he wanted to go there,
                                    desk, pen, paper, and all.

Then, she thought he meant he wanted to sketch
                                    his words onto the moon itself,
drawing a finger through the grainy, gray dust.

When he went to the window and wrote on the glass
where the moon hung stunned like a mark
            of terminal punctuation, she was surprised.

                        The cotton glowed white
as he drew the curtains closed, and the shadow
of his words rippled in the waves of the wind.

Valediction, On Arriving in a Distant Land

I am not one to travel with no destination. No city or continent
charms me with the vague glee of flight. Nor would I go alone,
for every day, we wake warmth to warmth, your breath in my ear,

my hand on your thigh. Yesterday, the planet bowed before us,
and cool distance clarified a curve measurable in miles, in feet
pacing dutifully through the world. I've crossed deserts and seas,

rivers and peaks from which the waters flow, the sun westering
and a moon pierced by sky while morning melts into noon. All
space intensifies, blue, absolute, definite and dismal, magnified

by our finite human measures when we mark our roads with signs
and lines and lights that regulate. Even now, with old mountains
at my back and a thin river lost in a valley of dust, I am with you.

The rays from stars cascade through darkness limitless and lit
too little. Light is slow beside the speed with which my thoughts
turn to you. And no world is large enough to come between us.

Posterity

From where I sit, the papaya reveals a bulbous ruff
of fruit swelling beneath a loose canopy of green
hands catching morning light.
                    The neighbor's new
roof gleams like a penny in light that might silver
if there were more, but the clouds return the rays
to the sky,
            bouncing them back into the universe
after an eight-minute flit from star to blue planet
and now, for eternity,
                a long, lightless rush through
space between stars that stars cannot illuminate.
Light seeks sand, sea, and mountains, to reflect on
some work of substance,
                to wring color from beams
full of rainbows and release one, an announcement
that of all of the colors the sun contains, this blue,
this red, this yellow,
                this green the eye entertains
is truly the only color this sky, this mango, these
bananas, and the ripening papaya
                do not accept.
And so, as this speck of earth arcs among the stars
around the prodigal sovereign of the sun,
                    we are
known by what we are not. Shadows cast black
contours where light falls, but leaves and legs
pass along gravel and grass
                as we do when the time
comes to rise and go, but the sun feeds the green
above and below the crown and heel,
                and the stars
light our way, and after we pass, the fruit golds
and falls, and only the sun burns for the earth.

Night Wildfire on the West Maui Mountains

Arcs of molten gold sketch the ridge: a black cloud
of rock scored with shining lines, a tiger whose stripes
       gleam in curves, a silhouette whose shadow

flickers with flame. This may be the way the beginning
looked or the end will appear--the island burning,

           rock ignited and rushing to the sea--
     in those final astonished seconds for scientists
who are too close, a red curtain across the landscape,

skin flaming like paper, vision boiled in the skull's cup,
bones exploding before burning, and not a moment

for another note, a photograph, or one last word.

Of Owls and Sugar Cane

Outraged, the local newspaper reports a tragic death of pueo,
            owl native to the islands, slammed from the sky
with fender, windshield, or grille. Yet a quick study of the photo

reveals a Barn Owl, limp with wing unfurled on a roadside
        where tall green stalks of cane rise behind the tidy pile

of feathers among the scattered trash. Of course, the bird
was a Barn Owl. They dive from the dark into headlights
          to strike mice the sudden day illuminates,

and drivers, eyes vacant with fatigue and too much familiarity
       with humming red roads, tear pale wings from stars

and cast hollow bones into the ditch. These drivers don't care
       what they hit and never stop to see. We are like them.

We won't know what's lost until we can name what we see.
       And we'll never know what will grow if we don't know

when or how to plant what the moon demands. Till the wheels
stop, we and our children will see no more in the earth but sugar
       and graves and the nameless grasses that cover them.

Five Planets at Once

"Come on outside," he said. "Tonight,
                    you can see five planets at once."

He was grinning, with the sort of secret a brother keeps.
        "There's no moon. They should be easy to see."

In the field, eye-deep in the night, he pointed into the dark.

"The big white one up there is Jupiter. Some people can see
            three or four moons without a telescope.
                    That butter-colored one is Saturn."

"There's Mars. It's a little faint, but if you look hard,
                    you can see the red color.
        The brilliant one right over the mountain is Venus."

Then, he was silent. We stared together at a sky glowing
                    with the other worlds ringing our sun.
        Wind and small animals rustled in the grass.

"Hey," I said, "I thought you said we could see five planets."
                                "We can."

"Well, look. Jupiter, Saturn, Mars, and Venus is only four."
                    "That's right."

I could hear the smile in his voice. I thought for a moment,
        but not long enough. "So what's the other one?"

            He chuckled, and said, "Earth."

What We Are

Faces our fingers touch are all we know of lovers. Flesh, blood, and bone
fill skin, but the skin is what we touch, and we think what we touch is all

there is, and all is well. Most of what matters is unseen. Waves on the sea
are most of what we know, yet the depths are most of what it is. The fire
of the sun we see is the surface, though that orb is full of light
          we never know.

The sky is a surface light creates with air, a blue curbing vision during day,
though night reveals millions of millennia and more of light beyond sleep.

Even the mountain we live on is known solely by shape, a surface familiar
yet fresh each day, for the mountain's face is all the mountain we know.
The heat in the heart is hidden, but for the flows fire forged into the slopes.

Five miles from root to peak, what makes the mountain massive is the rock
we cannot see beneath the sea. Surfaces are what we see. Depths are
          what we are.

Talking Some Sense into Myself: A Novena

Last Monday was the eighteenth anniversary of my mother's death.
My father, who demanded a decade ago I never speak to him again,
sent a Christmas card that arrived the same day. Peace on Earth.
Good will to whatever. Christ is born, one more lamb to the slaughter.
Well, I'm no innocent, and I'm out of a job. The letter came Tuesday,
my brother's birthday, the winter solstice, the darkest day of the year.
The radio fills the air with holiday music. Hark, the herald angels sing.

On Wednesday, three wise men sped past my house without a glance.
Thursday, rain fell. The roof boomed with the dead weight of water.
O, come, all ye faithful, joyful and triumphant. I watch the old dark spot
on the ceiling for leaks. It's starting to sink in. I don't have a job now,
and I'm not Shakespeare. I can't console myself with the easy myths
of immortality in the art and brats we make. Such a damn liar. He knew
there's only work to be done, and we need jobs for money to do the work.

Friday was Christmas Eve, my sister's birthday. The jolly, old elf skipped
my corrugated roof. On Christmas Day, the sun rose on wet, greening
grass I must cut soon. Deck the halls with boughs of holly. I need gas
for the mower and a clear, dry day for yard work. We stared all morning
at our tiny tree, rolled salami in tortillas, and watched someone else's
wonderful life unreel. There was alcohol to raise the Christmas spirits.

Sunday, no one rose. Monday, we bought bread, cheese, and coffee,
and returned some gifts for cash. On fifty TVs in housewares, smirking
anchors reported tens of thousands drowning in a tsunami on the day
after Christmas, brown waves spilling sand into the stark, blue jewels
of exclusive hotel pools. The footage rolls.

                                        Water flows through streets
and people climbing onto cars, roofs, each other. It's beginning to look
a lot like Christmas. Those fleeing crowds knew no more about life
than I do, but they knew enough to run when the big waves came, grew,
and flooded their houses, their shops, their lives, their lungs. The faces

reveal shock that the world can treat them this way. Mary, did you know? Yesterday, the sinking sun was a bloody smudge on the flat, gray wall of the horizon. If ever there was a good time to pull a Hemingway, this is it--to stamp my little foot one last time, curl a toe over the trigger, and have a blast. I have no job and no prospects. Surely, everyone will understand. Rudolph, with your nose so bright, won't you guide my sleigh tonight? At the kitchen table, I write my last cryptic notes toward a supreme fiction, drafting enough to leave behind some scraps of disappointment and wonder. Have yourself a merry, little Christmas.

Yet today, the death toll rose again, and suicide means the bastards win, little grins aglow behind folded hands praying eagerly for my damnation. Isn't it enough that any day can stuff your mouth with mud or drop a rock on your head as you clear a path through the park? And I'd never see a new year again, job or no job. The day is dark with clouds, and now, fog swallows our rented walls and windows. The road dims, disappears in a rolling, gray mist. I know the time, and I'm not going anywhere. Go, tell it on the mountain. Above the clouds, sunlight rains--I can't see it, but I know--like rocks from a blank sky. Already, the days grow longer.

iv. ka wanaʻao

dawn, the coming of the light, the time
of waking, rising, knowing

Arrival

When you arrive, on the sand among ironwood trees,
        the tides, and last light, you can almost see where you are,
and you see arrival is an idea about getting somewhere,

        yet the place you arrive was here long before you were,
but then it wasn't a place yet. And it's not that you are
        the center of the place, like a dumb jar lolling on a hilltop,

        but arriving draws a place together like a web, a set
        of radiating lines centering on you standing in the place,
looking around and finding a place to stand where every knot

        in the net sparkles like night suns waking over the black surge
of the sea. When you get to the place, your eyes start to focus,
        to find a point of view for the place to regard itself

through your eyes. The place urges words into the air like stars
        rising over the volcano. The place speaks with your voice,
        and the place makes you say, "Here, this is the place."

Luck and the Fisherman

When I see a man walk toward the shore,
carrying rod and tackle and buckets of bait,
or see another loading coolers in a boat,

filling the tank with gas and checking oil,
casting off lines, and stepping from dock
to deck, I never wish the fisherman luck.

Everyone knows the fish will catch our words
and scatter into tides and waves far beyond
hooks and lines and determination. The one

who wishes another good luck with fishing
gets a scowl and a curse, as the fisherman
turns his back on him and the sea for the day.

We greet the fishers with a smile and talk
of children or surf or lunch, of love or weather
or the long, noisy wars beyond the horizon,

but we never speak of the obvious. We never
wish luck to the those who are going fishing
so they may return with something big.

A Small Gathering of Light

The sun has yet to rise, but the silver sky has extinguished
      the stars. Haleakalā is black against the rising light.

      Maybe someone should say the mountain before dawn
is darker than the mountain at midnight under starlight. It is.
Last night, stars hovered at my fingertips. If there is fire,

      it is beyond me. On one side of the sky, Venus blazed
near Castor and Pollux. On the other, Jupiter brooded
          over the volcano. If light creates distance,

      then darkness draws us together. On nights when Venus
gleams on my right hand, and Jupiter on my left, I can't imagine
the world going on without me, but I am confident. It will.

With three nights yet to fill, the bold moon displays the face
          of change to us, journeying between the light
and its reflection. This morning, a single star shone to mark

      our direction. There is only a small gathering of light,
but with the mountain as a guide, any road through day will do.

Winter Storm Dawn

Wind rips through the trees, and the house creaks
like a redwood in winter. Little limbs tick on the walls,
      and ragged tarps on the neighbor's boat flap

against their ropes. Through the window, leaves are black
tatters in a torment of gray. Streetlights dim the valley,
      and the far ridge is a dark line between dawn

and rising rock. Not a rooster crows. Not a dog barks.
Storm haze blurs the edges of the neighborhood,
      and the stars are long gone, even from our hillside.

Above the tufts of cloud, a glow of rose illuminates
      tears in the folds of the storm. I know it's early,
but I wanted to wake you so you could see this light.

What I Least Expect

In the morning, what I can't expect is steak for breakfast
although I will take eggs, over easy, please, and some
chunked papaya. What I expect less is the barn owl

swooping from the kiawe tree and landing on the green
painted planks of the picnic table, pale, heart-shaped face

gaping and amazed. What I don't expect is the silence
spilling over the south field as the sun sets because
what I really do expect is the chittering of silverbills

and the slanting sparkle and spit of skylark song winding
through a blue too bright to spot him in. I never expect

to see the Black Francolin though I daily hear his piercing
call preceded by that clear thin whistle. Nor do I expect
to see the rim of Haleakalā after noon, but sometimes

that mad clarity remains all day till sunset pinks the slope.
And what I least expect, what I realize I never expect,

is whatever happens right in front of me as I walk uphill
on the fading two-track lane through knee-high grass
beyond the hibiscus bush and disappear over the crest.

Wasting Time on a Tuesday Morning

At the next table, the man's briefcase is open, and he annotates papers
with a plastic pen. He pauses and shakes it. He writes. He shakes
the pen, touches the point to his tongue, tries to write, then disgusted,

tosses it in the trashcan. He catches my look. "Out of ink," he says.
I nod, but this is not the least of his troubles. When next I glance

from the dregs of coffee etching dark lines in the bottom of my cup,
the man holds a lock the size of his thumb. His frown is ferocious,
but the lock is unmoved. He whirls the wheels and threatens the lock

beneath his breath. The lock is secure in its present position. Cursing,
he lobs the lock into the garbage. He glances at me, and I'm looking

again. "Forgot the combination." If only that were the end of all this.
When I return from refilling my cup, he glares at his watch. The time

the watch displays is the same the clock behind him on the wall conveys,
an honest face so open I believe it. He removes the watch, looks again:
same time, same sincere expression, same precisely arranged hands.

The seconds sweep his life away like dust from a coffee shop sidewalk.
He flips the watch and examines the stainless steel circle. No time there.

No reflection. He looks once more at the face and pitches the watch
in the can. He turns to me and says, "She left me." So that's it. I rattle
the paper, sip my coffee, weigh the news. I still have plenty of time.

Illumination

On those cold, clear winter mornings, I rise in the dark and sit
      beneath a lamp with a pen and paper in a circle of light
barely bright enough for the work. The window beside me is black

and blank, and soon I'm staring only through the window of the page
at whatever I'm drawing from ink and concentration. Hours pass,
      and always, when I least expect it, there's a sudden tide of light

as the sun crests the mountain. When the first rays flood the fields,
the thin, yellow curtain behind me brightens, and the room swells
      with light. Everything is suddenly golden and illuminated,

and for just that one moment, I make the glorious and forgivable
      mistake of thinking it has something to do with me.

Dark Green

All is halved, and half is always hidden. Dawn glows
in a perfect pink sky of beginnings while the green side
of the mountain darkens beneath the cloudy ragged ridge.

In this half light, the cardinal in the jacaranda burns red.
His call for his mate pierces morning. Our lives are lit
by the sun, yet half of every day is dark. Watch closely

what comes. Yesterday, a rare storm loosed loud torrents,
and sorrow struck like sunlight through a rip in rainclouds.

A rainbow bent through the blue, but the other half sank
in the soil, and now, the land revives. This mystery is old
and never welcome. From hidden roots, raw strength rises.

Lifting life to light, a tide flows through trunk and branch,
forces buds into the world's broken half. Remember this:
the darkness drawn from earth makes the new leaves green.

The Witch's House

The witch's house has a roof of grass, tall seeded stalks, wild,
      wound with light in the wind, over walls of rutted red earth.
Her windows are lit by day and darken at night. The witch's house

      stands atop the only hill to the north, stark against the sky,
on the blue edge of the only horizon we see from the village below.
The witch summons the townsfolk to visit her daily, and they go,

wending the narrow trail on the gentle slope of gray, half-buried
boulders and grass and cows of black and white. The children run
through narrow cobbled lanes with sticks and hoops and barking
      dogs and the shrieks and shouted words that only children

understand. At night, many of the villagers return, plodding, weary,
some weeping, and all eager to lock the world beyond their bolted
doors. When at last I forget my birthday too, I meander along

      the stone-lined path to the witch's door, and when I cross
the rough-hewn threshold so many have passed before me,
the house is empty. Sunlight brightens the red and blue spiral

of the kitchen rug and gleams on the polished stove and crockery.
The narrow bed is neat, beneath a quilt knotted with the elegant,
embroidered images of birds and beasts. The only closet is closed.
      The yellow curtains are tied back with artful knots of bows,

framing the pale and pretty landscape I neglect again to view.
The hearth is brilliant with flames of red and gold, and the stones
are swept and tidy near the trim iron tools kept to cultivate fire.

The witch is not at home, nor do I see any of the visitors I expect.
The armchair I choose is as soft as silence within cheerful walls,
      and I think the witch's house is empty until I remember.

The Piety in Weeding

Every Sunday, the gardener is on his knees, head bowed
beneath the yellow eye of all that looks down on him.
He enters the garden with a straw halo, steel fork, trowel,

shears, and downcast eyes. His righteousness in weeding
appalls, despite the duty that drives the work, but he is here.
Bent on the lawn, sun wringing sweat from reddened skin,

his fingers seek what he will cast aside. The weeds, hardy
and adventurous, are torn singly from the heedless land.
The gardener strains to clear each green inch of the acres

he claims for one clan of blades alone. His hands brown
with earth, his nails black with toil and dedication, he seeks
those who do not belong and executes each with a ropy grip

and deft flick of the wrist. He tosses root, stem, and flower
into a heap of steaming green and turns to the next invader,
marking his dripping brow with a thoughtless streak of dirt.

His fingers tug, twist, and tear at what he refuses to let live,
these thin, pale roots driving desperately into the ground,
clinging to the sandy soil as if they had a right to be there.

Hōkū Grades My Students' Poems

The crinkle and tatter of paper as she gyres through pages
is her joy in this assignment. Metaphors don't move her,

nor does fancy font on a perfumed, pink page. She rolls
on her back among poems, a wriggle of ecstasy sparked
by sun on her upturned belly. It's Fall, classes are begun,

and windows that don't admit the summer sun are open
to morning light slanting across the table and the words
my students offer the world. Hōkū sniffs the tidy edges

of blurred sheets, creasing pages as she rubs herself chin
to chest over the lines. When the branches outside move,

she leaps and spits at the shadows of leaves, and a rasp
of paper is the only voice Hōkū hears in her ruminations
on Emily's light verse and Steven's lax and adjectival ode

to his own broken heart. Before I stop her, Hōkū slashes
a villanelle about chickens and another Bishop-spawned

sestina on grandmothers. But I'm the one who rips in two
the first page of an odd homage to Ginsberg's *Howl* as I pull
the paper from beneath her manic, green-eyed symposium.

Her circles as she chases her tail over the sun-warmed table
are comic when our little literature flies in all directions,
but soon, she's asleep in a litter of verse and scattered leaves.

Beneath her paw, she's bent one corner of a page as perfectly
as a reader who wishes to remember where to begin again.

How to Make a Lei

an epithalamion for Lisa and J.D.

Stand beneath the stars at dawn, and as light rises, gather a scatter
of blossoms from beneath the plumeria tree. Sometimes, enough
have fallen to the grass, sometimes not. For the rest, cup each flower

in your fingers to warm the stem, and wait. Most will stay, but some
few blooms release the limb and come easily to hand. Only what is
freely given is worth receiving. Carry the blossoms to the kitchen table,

and arrange them before the work begins. A design will soon emerge
from the flowers you've found. Place every blossom within the circle,
and place each one well. Cut a thread. Count an inch for each week

of the year, and for grace, add the span of your hand. A little slack
is the measure we save for luck. Loop the line around a pen, chopstick,
scissors, whatever comes to hand. Through each five-petaled bloom,

guide a light thread through the golden heart, one flower at a time,
until a ribbon of blossoms lays before you, then tie a knot that draws
the ends together. To present the lei, ask your love to close both eyes

as we do for a first kiss. Such a moment renews the memory. Lower
the garland, and whisper of love. Above all, as you weave your ring
of flowers through morning, contemplate the face and heart of the one

for whom the work is done. Ponder long the lesson of the plumeria,
subtle as the gentle scent: the blossoms last only a day, but the making
of the lei endures all through our lives. Make as many as you may.

Even Further West

There is no jay in the shrinking alphabet of birds on Maui.
No madrone, but there is kiawe and ten thousand shades

of green creeping from red volcanic soil. The mountain is

not holy, but I worship all I see. Holy is a bamboo cage
in the human head, where the mind flutters. A mountain
shaped by fire and wind and rain and the mortal machines

of men is only what you can't think it is. Sacred is best
left unsaid. Every place is sacred, but thinking so never

makes it so. The mind. All a joke. Holiness. A smug pun.
Here, try this. Show me the Buddha, and I will make him
disappear. Try again. Once more, gone. Hands are easy

to empty. The mind, not so much. Here's a red feather

from a cardinal, a cowrie from the south shore. Hold them
till your hand cramps. Hold them till your mind changes.

Notes

The Edge of Where I'm Welcome: The Hawaiian archipelago is the most remote place in the world, two thousand miles from any continental land mass.

Cardinal in February: O'ahu: Plumeria is a fragrant, five-petaled flower, in colors from white to cream to gold and more, also known as frangipani.

Witnesses: The mountain and the volcano are one and the same, always Haleakalā, the House of the Sun, on Maui.

Redemption: Li hing mui powder is a red, grainy spice made from the skins of dried, salted plums and sugar. The powder is sprinkled on a wide variety of candy, fruit, and other treats and sweets, and in this case, on a frozen cherry slushy drink from Byron's (a local drive-in restaurant once near the airport and now closed forever).

On the Set of Lost: All episodes of the television series *Lost* were reportedly shot exclusively in the Hawaiian islands and at least once on the campus of Honolulu Community College.

Upcountry Overlook: Kula, Maui: Kiawe is the algoroba tree, a type of mesquite.

All There Is: An epithalamion is a poem written in celebration of a wedding. The two true seasons in the islands are the dry season and the rainy season. The dry season lasts from May through September; the rainy season lasts from October through April. The only other season of note is the hurricane season, which lasts from June through November.

Letter to Slow Cooker in Colorado: When Chief Joseph of the Nez Perce tribe surrendered to the forces of General Oliver Howard on October 5, 1877, he spoke these words: "From where the sun now stands, I will fight no more forever."

Sitting in the Last of Sunset, Listening to Guests Within: The owl hovering in the last of the light on the sunset slope of Haleakalā is pueo, the endemic Short-eared Owl, also known as the Hawaiian Owl.

Picnic in the Year Zero: Where the sky starts is a matter of guesswork and purposes, but the Kármán line, about sixty miles up, is a common demarcation for where our atmosphere fades into outer space. Ray Milland is the star of the classic science-fiction film *Panic in the Year Zero*, another Cold-War-era B-movie presenting a lovingly rendered Hollywood apocalypse.

Talking Some Sense into Myself: A Novena: A novena is a personal and public devotional prayer of nine days for the purposes of mourning, preparation for an approaching feast, petition, or forgiveness.

What I Least Expect: According to the local bird book, the Black Francolin, a secretive quail-like bird whose call is heard everywhere upcountry, but whose face is rarely seen, was introduced from India in 1959. The Gray Francolin, a more commonly seen upcountry resident, introduced from India in 1958, has a long, piercing call, louder than a rooster's and much more musical. For me, the Gray Francolin is the voice of Kula, and the Black Francolin is its heart.

The Witch's House: A landform on the southwestern horizon and visible from the desk where I write, the witch's house is an accidental artifact of perspective and landscape. Still, I didn't notice until Veronica showed me that one hillock resembles a squat, little house with a tall, thin chimney. She remembered a similar feature from the mountains where she had been raised in Indonesia, saying that the childhood thought of the witch's house nearby had always been pleasantly scary. I began to speculate on who lived at the edge of the sky and why.

Even Further West: A cowrie is the speckled or striped egg-shaped shell of a sea snail or other marine mollusc.

Acknowledgments

Grateful acknowledgment is made to the editors of the following publications, in which these poems are forthcoming, first published, or reprinted.

2010 Lorin Tarr Gill Writing Competition for Poetry (First Place): A Boat of Bones

Bamboo Ridge: Illumination; Samson; Someone Else's Beach

Blue Collar Review: Of Owls and Sugar Cane; Talking Some Sense into Myself: A Novena

Cider Press Review: Posterity

Coe Review: A Small Gathering of Light

Connecticut Review: The Floor God

Cordite Poetry Review (Australia): What I'll Miss When I'm Gone

CV2 (Canada): What We Are

Dalhousie Review (Canada): All There Is

Gargoyle: Picnic in the Year Zero

Going Down Swinging (Australia): Headlights: A Biology Lesson; Letter to Slow Cooker in Colorado; The Lone Streetlight on Piliwale Road; Redemption

Hawai'i Pacific Review: Night Wildfire on the West Maui Mountains

Hawai'i Review: Cardinal in February: O'ahu; The Lone Streetlight on Piliwale Road

The Hollins Critic: An Inflatable Globe for Your Birthday

Iota (England): To Write on the Moon

Island (Australia): Arrival; Even Further West

Jack London Is Dead: Contemporary Euro-American Poetry of Hawai'i (And Some Stories): On the Set of *Lost*

Lummox: My Potatoes, Too

Magma (England): A Humanity of Glass; Wasting Time on a Tuesday Morning

MARGIE: Weather Eye

Maui Muses (Volume 3): Dogs, Men, and Fences in Fog

Maui Muses: Equitude (Volume 4): An Inflatable Globe for Your Birthday; Maybe

Oregon Literary Review: On the Day the World Ends; Witnesses

Poetry East: Too Dark to Read

Poetry NZ (New Zealand): How to Make a Lei

RATTLE: For My Sake; Telephone Lines; Valediction, On Arriving in a Distant Land

River Oak Review: The Floor God

Seawords: Arrival; Luck and the Fisherman; What We Are

Slant: Luck and the Fisherman

Slate: Sitting in the Last of Sunset, Listening to Guests Within

Snowy Egret: Dogs, Men, and Fences in Fog

SOUTH Poetry Magazine (England): On My Father's Wish That I Not Attend His Funeral

Southword Journal (Ireland): Hōkū Grades My Students' Poems; A Small Gathering of Light; The Witch's House

The Stand Magazine (England): Cardinal in February: O'ahu; The Piety in Weeding

Sugar House Review: Winter Storm Dawn

The Sun Magazine: Illumination

Takahē (New Zealand): A Constant Line of Ants Through Night

Tampa Review: What Rain Brings to the Volcano

Tar River Poetry: All There Is; The Way of Feet

Think Journal: Dark Green

Turtle Island Quarterly: What I Least Expect

Weber: The Contemporary West: The Edge of Where I'm Welcome; Five
    Planets at Once; Maybe; Upcountry Overlook: Kula, Maui

Westerly (Australia): Streamside; Walking Zone

Gratitude

As I have elsewhere and I do daily, I thank my many fellow writers for good advice and good will through the years, especially Tony Alcantara and Matt Daly, who in recent years have made my writing better and my thinking clearer.

Thanks to Melinda Gohn for "the floor god" writing prompt and to her and the many members of the Maui Live Poets Society for years of good fellowship.

Thanks to my many publishers: James Taylor III, at Longhand Press; Jordan Jones, at Leaping Dog Press; Donald Allen, at Grey Fox Press; Paul Rosheim, at Obscure Publications, and Ginny Connors, at Grayson Books.

As always, I thank every first and last member of the Ancient Order of the Fire Gigglers, beginning with our founder Lew Welch and especially including the fine writers, good friends, and local charter members James Taylor III, John Kain, and Kathryn Capels.

As my dark memory directs, I offer special thanks to everyone I haven't named here but who was essential to everything: you know who you are.

And to Veronica Winegarner, my spouse, my friend, my companion, and my partner in every manner of mischief, I give my greatest thanks and all my love.

About the Author

Eric Paul Shaffer is author of six books of poetry, including *A Million-Dollar Bill*; *Lāhaina Noon*; *Portable Planet*; and *Living at the Monastery, Working in the Kitchen*.

More than 450 of his poems have been published in the USA, Australia, Canada, England, Ireland, Japan, New Zealand, Nicaragua, Scotland, and Wales. Shaffer received Hawai'i's 2002 Elliot Cades Award for Literature, a 2006 Ka Palapala Po'okela Book Award for *Lāhaina Noon*, the 2009 James M. Vaughan Award for Poetry, and first place in the 2010 Lorin Tarr Gill Writing Competition for Poetry.

He received a fellowship to attend the 2006 Summer Fishtrap Writers Workshop, was a visiting poetry faculty member at the 23rd Annual Jackson Hole Writers Conference in 2015, and has been an occasional guest faculty member, delivering the Keynote Address in 2013, at the Ko'olau Writers Workshops, offered annually by Hawai'i Pacific University.

Shaffer teaches composition, literature, and creative writing at Honolulu Community College.

Other Books

Poetry

Kindling: Poems from Two Poets
Longhand Press, with James Taylor III

RattleSnake Rider
Longhand Press

Portable Planet
Leaping Dog Press

Living at the Monastery, Working in the Kitchen
Leaping Dog Press

Lāhaina Noon: Nā Mele O Maui
Leaping Dog Press

Road Sign Suite: Across America and Again
Obscure Publications

Restoring ~~Lady~~ Liberty
Obscure Publications

A Million-Dollar Bill
Grayson Books

Fiction

You Are Here
Obscure Publications

The Felony Stick
	Leaping Dog Press

Burn & Learn, or Memoirs of the Cenozoic Era
	Leaping Dog Press

Criticism

How I Read Gertrude Stein by Lew Welch
	Grey Fox Press

Printed in the USA
CPSIA information can be obtained
at www.ICGtesting.com
CBHW031120231023
1466CB00004B/139